DEALING WITH BULLYING

BY HOLLY DUHIG

BookLife
PUBLISHING

©2018
BookLife Publishing
King's Lynn
Norfolk PE30 4LS

A catalogue record for this
book is available from the
British Library.

ISBN: 978-1-78637-291-8

Written by:
Holly Duhig

Edited by:
Kirsty Holmes

Designed by:
Danielle Rippengill

All facts, statistics, web addresses and URLs in this book were verified as valid and accurate at time of writing.
No responsibility for any changes to external websites or references can be accepted by either the author or publisher.

KIN

Please renew or return items by the date
shown on your receipt

www.hertfordshire.gov.uk/libraries

Renewals and enquiries: 0300 123 4049

Textphone for hearing or 0300 123 4041
speech impaired users:

L32 11.16

527 612 90 9

CONTENTS

WORDS THAT LOOK LIKE **THIS** CAN BE FOUND IN THE GLOSSARY ON PAGE 24.

DEALING WITH BULLYING

My name is Rueben, and I've been bullied. Being bullied was horrible. It made me feel scared and very alone.

It all started when James joined my school. He had been <u>excluded</u> from his old school because he was badly behaved and didn't like being told what to do.

James started picking on me in front of my friends. He would call me names and kick my stuff. Everyone was scared of James, so my friends started picking on me too.

NOBODY WANTED TO PLAY WITH ME ANYMORE.

Every time I got good marks on my homework, James would make everyone call me "teacher's pet". When I cried, he called me a weakling.

ARGUMENTS AND BULLYING

Sometimes, friends fall out or have arguments. I fell out with my friend, Erica, because we were arguing about what to watch on TV. She called me names but said sorry straight away afterwards.

This made me feel sad, but it wasn't bullying. Bullying makes you feel sad for a long time. Bullying is when people do hurtful things over and over again.

JAMES USED TO SNAP MY PENS AND PENCILS EVERY DAY.

At School 🍎

I used to enjoy school but James made me feel scared to go.

My School

Some mornings I felt really sick. I tried to tell Mum that I couldn't go to school that day because I was ill. She took my **temperature** but I was fine. Not too hot, or too cold.

Mum asked me if I was worried about something, but I couldn't tell her about James. It felt too **embarrassing**.

School made me miserable. The only times I felt really happy were on Saturdays when I had football practice.

The friends I have on my football team don't go to my school so it's really fun! My next-door neighbour and best friend, Aaron, also goes to football.

Telling a Grown-Up

After a while, though, I couldn't even have fun at football.

I couldn't concentrate because I was busy worrying about school on Monday. My coach asked me if there was anything bothering me.

I told him all about the bullying at school. It made me cry. My coach told me it was normal to feel sad when someone is picking on you. It doesn't make you weak to ask for help.

Talking to Mum

Next time I felt sick before school, I realised it was because I was scared of James. I decided to tell Mum all about what was happening at school.

Mum said I should make a list of all the things that James had done. This would make it easier to tell my teacher what had been happening.

TELLING MY TEACHER

Mum came with me to tell my teacher, Ms. Hutchins.

MS. HUTCHINS

I was worried she wouldn't believe me, but she did. She said she would talk to James and let him know that bullying is <u>unacceptable</u>.

James had made me feel like it was babyish to complain about being bullied. It took a lot of **courage** to tell people about it.

Ms. Hutchins made James **apologise** to me for everything he'd done. I asked him why he chose to pick on me.

James said he was bullied at his old school for not being clever enough. He thought that if he picked on me, people wouldn't notice that he wasn't doing well in class.

I felt sorry for James, but it was still not fair to bully me.
I'm glad I stood up to him in the end.

NOBODY SHOULD BE MADE TO FEEL BAD ABOUT WHO THEY ARE.

I am much happier at school now and I have lots of friends because people aren't scared of James anymore. We know the right way to stand up for ourselves.

Glossary and Index

Glossary

apologise	to express regret for something you have done wrong
courage	being able to do something that frightens you
embarrassing	when something makes you feel awkward, self-conscious or ashamed
excluded	no longer allowed to attend school
temperature	how hot a person, place or object is
unacceptable	not allowed or bad

Index